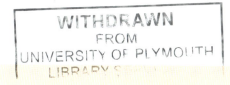

.AN THOMAS's
lected Poems

Reflections from the classroom

is a series which has been published by the National Language Unit of Wales, a section of the Welsh Joint Education Committee, in response to requests from teachers of English who are keen to include writing from Wales within the selection of texts offered to their students.

Sandra Anstey
Series Editor
WJEC National Language Unit of Wales

Stephen M Rees is Head of English at Llanishen High School, Cardiff

Thanks to **Jeff Towns** of Dylans Bookstore, Swansea, for permission to include the photographs of Dylan Thomas which appear on pages 27-28.

NATIONAL LANGUAGE UNIT OF WALES
——— WJEC / CBAC ———
UNED IAITH GENEDLAETHOL CYMRU

Designed by Tracy Davies

Published by
WJEC National Language Unit
245/251 Western Avenue
Cardiff CF5 2YX

© WJEC National Language Unit
1998
All rights reserved

ISBN 1 86085 290 4

Contents

Introduction	3
To begin at the beginning	4
Man, myth and reputation	5
Starting points	8
Looking at titles	8
From titles to extracts	9
Contrast and comparison	12
Ways through 70 poems	13
Collection by collection	13
Themes	14
Approaches to individual poems	18
'Prologue'	18
'And death shall have no dominion'	20
'The force that through the green fuse'	21
'Once it was the colour of saying'	22
'In my craft or sullen art'	23
'Do not go gentle into that good night'	24
Critical responses	25
Assignments	29
Bibliography	30
Index of approaches	32
Index of poems cited	32

Cover of *Dylan Thomas, Selected Poems,* edited by Walford Davies
(Everyman, 1993)

Introduction

The Japanese have a process whereby a living person can be designated a national treasure: we British seem to prefer ours dead and preferably made of masonry. A Welsh building like Cardiff Castle is clearly part of the National Heritage, but a Welsh person ...?

A radical and adventurous director of an ageing institution in London once said that he would have found his job of getting new people into his building much easier if he didn't have three of the most off-putting words in the title of the place: "Imperial" and "War" and "Museum". In other words, preconceptions play an important part in how we appreciate things, so that "Dylan Thomas the Welsh Poet" comes – for some – with a whole range of responses built up over the years .

In the classroom, however, Dylan Thomas can be a new experience; the images which some university students of literature and teachers have of the man and his poetry may mean little or nothing to some of our A level students.

My approach to the presentation of the poems of Dylan Thomas in the classroom recognises the difficulties inherent in the teaching of a substantial selection of the work of any poet, and also uses the sense of newness which young students bring to the classroom experience of literature to make the exploration of the poems something which is useful and rewarding – for teachers as well as students.

I have used what I hope are fairly gentle exercises by way of an introduction to Thomas's work, linking poetry and biography, progressing through titles and extracts to suggestions for the analysis of whole poems.

The seventy poems by Dylan Thomas which comprise *Selected Poems* (Everyman, 1993), a set text for the WJEC A level English Literature syllabus, is a substantial number for students to encompass – probably as many as they have had to respond to during the whole of their previous schooling; the classroom teacher has to be sensitive to the responses that this weight of poetry will produce. Realistically, everyone makes selections. I hope that the approaches here will allow teachers and pupils to make their personal choices and enjoy the study of a poet who said of himself, "I wanted to write poetry in the beginning because I had fallen in love with words" *(Texas Quarterly*, Winter 1961 [1951]).

Stephen M Rees
Llanishen High School
Cardiff

To begin at the beginning...

When Lord Byron's poem 'The Corsair' was published in 1814 it sold an estimated 10,000 copies in one day. It has been a long time since a British poet was a sensational popular best seller on this scale. The popularity of the poem has sunk – though lyrics, advertising jingles and internet doggerel keep the format alive and thriving. The most popular single literary form is now prose – short story, article or novel – and, in the classroom, the introduction of a book of poems can be greeted with muted enthusiasm.

I find that it pays to get the intellectual opposition out in the classroom straight away. Initial thoughts can be springboards into productive work, sometimes because of their negative aspect rather than in spite of it.

As a way of recording the process of discussion and the developing responses to the texts, I encourage my students to keep a record of their work on poetry. I find that this recording can most easily be facilitated by the use of a drafting book where brain-stormed ideas, quick responses and first drafts of formal exercises can all be written down and preserved as a record of the process of study.

I recently asked a new A level class what response they had to the word poetry and what they expected from poetry itself: the reaction was mixed and a brain-stormed list was soon produced which included:

Difficulty	Rhythm
Puzzles	Funny language
Verses	Different perspectives
Weird subjects	Short lines
Rhyme	Words and phrases
Something about nothing	that were easy to remember

This list led on to a class discussion which picked up on those aspects which seemed strange or difficult to the students, and developed into a consideration of **subject matter** - where the title of the poem did not seem to link to the content; **personal response** - the difficulty that students had in appreciating the quality of a poem whose subject matter did not really interest them; **persona** - the confusion of the poet as a writer with the character speaking within the poem; **use of language and poetic form** - the perennial problem for many students of why anyone would want to write in such an odd form using such difficult language.

This was a very productive exercise and allowed me to introduce a prepared range of short poems on the overhead projector which challenged some of the negative assumptions made by my students. I used the lyrics of a current pop song, an advertising jingle, a limerick, a birthday card message, a Blake poem, some comic poems. The verse was chosen for its immediacy, its simplicity and the obvious use of rhyme, rhythm and imagery. The students were able to respond easily and the discussion was interesting and useful.

This exercise can obviously be conducted across the age range and students can be asked to collect examples of verse from everyday sources for use in class: their own favourite poems, lyrics, newspaper obituaries, birthday messages, magazine poems and advertisements.

The discussion then moved on to Welshness: what makes/made the Welsh specifically Welsh and Wales specifically Wales? (See Jude Brigley's *Approaches to the Study of Stories from Wales* and Mark Powell and

Mike Ross's *Approaches to the Study of Poems from Wales* – both titles in this series – for a similar introductory approach.)

Ideas were explored through brainstorming and a long list was produced.

From there we moved to a discussion of nationality. What effects could nationality have on a poet's writings?

These activities – with the focus on poetry and Welshness – provided a fertile beginning for an exploration of Dylan Thomas's poems.

MAN, MYTH AND REPUTATION

Dylan Thomas has become almost a mythic figure in the literature of Wales, Britain and the world – but such an image is not shared by all students when they start their A level studies. A teacher's appeal to a memory of the rich, distinctive voice, the curly-headed Augustus John portrait, Richard Burton's interpretation as First Voice, the famous bits of poems may well fall on deaf and uncomprehending ears.

Towards the end of Dylan Thomas's life (and during a greater part of it) both the public and Thomas himself worked to perpetuate the hard drinking, hard living, rough genius image. After his death the Thomas industry continued to flourish with fact, fiction, myth, magic and aspiration all mixing and clouding the literary achievement of the poet at the expense of the biography.

There is a wealth of material to present to a class which deals with the eventful life of Dylan Thomas. Students who are encouraged to

research Thomas will find a range of books which offer various versions of the life of the poet. It is important, therefore, that students learn to develop a critical sense which is able to distinguish the sensational and hagiographical from the reasonable and balanced.

An approach that I have used when focusing on various literary characters is to present students with a variety of biographies of their subject and to use these as a basis for discussion about presentation; trying to distinguish fact from opinion, reasonable commentary from rewriting history.

The following general questions offer a starting point:

Who was Dylan Thomas?

What do you know of the man?

What have you heard or what do you know about his character?

What sorts of things did Thomas write?

If, as is likely, little is known by your students then I have found it useful to present them with the biographical extracts and accompanying prompts which follow.

● Read through the brief biographies on the next page and find one or two more from your own library research.

● As you read through think about or make notes on the following:

What factual information does each biography give?

What seems to be the most important focus of each biography?

What sort of language is used to describe Thomas?

What significant differences are there in these biographies?

What impression of Thomas do you get from each?

What judgements are being made?

What opinions are being expressed?

Which one of them do you find the most interesting/balanced/intriguing?

● In what ways are the brief biographies presenting Dylan Thomas to their readers?

● Compare the material you have just read with the brief chronology found in the 1993 Everyman edition of Dylan Thomas's *Selected Poems* (pages xxxix-xli).

● How far does the information found in the Everyman chronology match the brief biographies?

If you were to present a biography of Dylan Thomas to the rest of the class, as an introduction to the study of his writing, consider how you would use the information contained in your sources (brief biographies plus extra library references) to complete this task.

Which sources would you find the most useful?

Which sources would you reject?

Which sources would you modify?

Which sources would you trust?

What other information do you think you would need?

Welsh poet with a hard drinking, boisterous reputation. His poems are exuberant, often florid and occasionally obscure. His best-known single work is *Under Milk Wood* (1954), a radio drama in poetic prose.

Dictionary of Biography (Brockhampton Press, 1995)

Welsh poet. He worked as a journalist in Wales before moving to London in 1934, in which year his book of poems *18 Poems* appeared. He rapidly acquired a reputation as a hard drinking, boisterous pub poet, which, combined with his exuberant, florid and occasionally obscure verse, created a lived-up-to persona which ultimately led to his death (in New York). His own recordings of his work are superb. His first collected edition, *Collected Poems* (1952), sold over 30,000 copies in its first year. His best-known single work is *Under Milk Wood* (1954), a radio drama in poetic prose that is regarded as a milestone in broadcasting.

Edwin Moore, Editor*, Dictionary of Literature* (Geddes and Grosset, 1992)

Welsh poet, writer and broadcaster whose 'welsh-singing' voice enraptured millions in his readings of his own and other verse. He worked on a Welsh newspaper, but gained immediate recognition as a poet with *18 Poems* (1934), when he was only 20. The lyric quality of his verse was outstanding, and *The Map of Love* (1939), *Portrait of the Artist as a Young Dog* (1940), *The World I Breathe* (1940), *Deaths and Entrances* (1946), *Poems* (1950) and *The Doctor and the Devils*, a film script (1953), established him, but it was *Under Milk Wood* which gained him real fame. This remarkable work originated as a radio play script about a Welsh seaside village, entitled *Quite Early One Morning*, which Dylan Thomas expanded into the fine *Under Milk Wood* - but tragically, it was not published as such until 1954, after his death in New York from cirrhosis of the liver. The work was full of fun and fresh, vivid similes, and it had much lyric tenderness it has also been adapted as a highly successful play. Also published posthumously (1955) were *Adventures in the Skin Trade*, an unfinished novel, and *A Prospect by the Sea*, edited by D Jones. Dylan Thomas was hailed by the critics: Edith Sitwell eulogised his poetry; Toynbee called him '"the greatest living poet in the English language'"; Sir Herbert Read, '"the most absolute poetry written in our time". But when he died a joint British-American fund had to be launched for the support of his widow and three children.

The New Universal Library Volume 5 (Caxton, 1967)

Starting points

There is no one way of starting a study of poetry, but, in the approaches that I have tried, I am aware that, when studying Dylan Thomas's poems for examination within the current A level syllabus, students are required to read and appreciate seventy poems – a daunting task for most. My approach, therefore, has been to encourage the students to become familiar with limited aspects of the poetry and begin to use the titles of poems before they have developed a detailed knowledge of the poetry itself.

LOOKING AT TITLES

Although dictionaries of quotations are edited by individuals whose opinions influence the final selection, their avowed intent is to reflect what has passed into general use, what is popular and lasts in the public's mind.

Popularity is no guarantee of worth and, as "A Mars a day helps you work, rest and play" is one of the most memorable jingles of recent years, poetic profundity does not always match survival, but, ruthless though it is, what dictionaries of quotations deem significant can indicate a rough guide to importance.

The following exercise uses those poem titles by Dylan Thomas which reappear in a selection of dictionaries of quotations. I have found it useful to prepare a list of these titles and then distribute it to students for their responses. As this is an introductory exercise I have used it over a single lesson: it can be as the basis for class response, group response or for individual work.

- Read through the following poem titles.

- In a sentence write what you think each poem is about.

- Which is the most memorable title? Why?

- Make brief notes of your response in your drafting books.

'Do not go gentle into that good night'

'Fern Hill'

'The force that through the green fuse drives the flower'

'A Refusal to Mourn the Death, by Fire, of a Child in London'

'And death shall have no dominion'

'The hand that signed the paper'

'Poem in October'

'Light breaks where no sun shines'

This is a brief and fairly light exercise which can then lead on to consideration of all the titles in *Selected Poems*.

A way of tackling all the titles is to photocopy the seventy in the selection and then cut the sheets into strips, one title per strip. The students can then be divided into groups and given a random selection of the titles with the task of responding to the following prompts:

- Offer suggestions for the content of a poem with this title.

- Give one word to describe the effect of the poem's title on you.

- In what ways (if any) does this title sound like a poem's title?

One group had the following selection of titles: 'The force that through the green fuse'; 'Once it was the colour of saying'; 'I have longed to move away'; 'Poem'; 'Out of a war of wits'.

Their suggestions for possible subject matter ranged from "terrorism" to "unrequited love". Their single word responses were "obvious", "bizarre", "interesting" and "silly" while their suggestions for the 'poetic' nature of the titles mentioned metaphor and intense personal experience.

Group responses fed back to the class so that there was a general discussion about the range and expectations of students. I was pleased that my students were able to suggest links between titles that one group had discussed with those of another group. Some groups even developed a sort of 'happy families' approach where they traded titles to make their group of titles more homogeneous.

Responses were noted so that they could be checked against future readings of the poems.

FROM TITLES TO EXTRACTS

I then asked my students to read and respond to the opening lines of a selection of poems. I gave them the sample sheet which appears on page 10 to show one way of responding to the given material.

I next gave them a sheet following the format which appears on page 11. I reminded the students about the work that they had already completed and the themes and ideas that they had identified. I emphasised that they might find it helpful to respond to some of the following points:

- the title of the poem

- key words or significant vocabulary

- imagery

- content

- expectations

- the form of the poem

- personal response.

These sheets could be completed individually or in groups with a feedback session to allow responses to be shared. The purpose of this exercise was to get students to respond to the actual poetry of Thomas, but in a brief form so that a relatively rapid response was possible.

The choice of poems to introduce at this point is, of course, up to the individual teacher and the composition of classes; variations of the sheet are easy to produce and this approach can be extended to any poems in the collection.

An unexpected title leads into a poem which poses a number of questions. What power does the stranger have? As 'Love' is in the title, does it apply to the 'girl'? The use of slang gives a colloquial feel, and the exuberant image suggests vitality rather than disturbance.

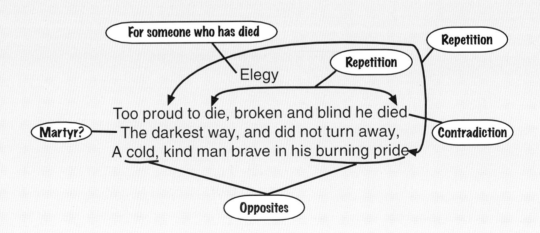

The title tells us that the subject of the poem is dead, and did not die an easy death. The harsh words give a strong sense of suffering and force questions. The adjectives used are odd: 'cold' and 'kind', 'brave' and 'darkest' – the dead man seems to have died for a cause, almost as if he was a martyr.

DYLAN THOMAS's
Selected Poems

When you respond to these extracts do not be afraid to make notes on the sheet itself: underline, link, note, think. You might find it helpful to think about the title, key words, significant vocabulary, imagery, content, expectations, form, personal response – or anything else which seems important to you.

The hand that signed the paper

The hand that signed the paper felled a city;
Five sovereign fingers taxed the breath,
Doubled the globe of dead and halved a country;
These five kings did a king to death.

I see the boys of summer

I see the boys of summer in their ruin
Lay the gold tithings barren,
Setting no store by harvest, freeze the soils;
There in their heat the winter floods
Of frozen loves they fetch their girls,
And drown the cargoed apples in their tides.

CONTRAST AND COMPARISON

I have found it useful to present two extracts from Dylan Thomas's writing for comparison as a starting-point for discussion of key aspects of Thomas's content and style. There are many possible combinations here, but in my experience setting lines of poetry against prose offers many similarities and differences which provoke lively discussions.

The questions which follow (some devised by me, others added by students) have proved helpful here.

> Which is the easier to respond to?
>
> Which do you prefer?
>
> What are the points of contact?
>
> What are the points of difference?
>
> Where is the narrator in each?
>
> What points of comparison are there in the use of language?
>
> What types of images are used?
>
> How appropriate do you find the use of images?
>
> How successful do you find these pieces of writing?
>
> Do you feel like reading on?

During a recent comparison of 'The hunchback in the park' and the opening of the story entitled 'The Mouse and the Woman', my students began by commenting on the two titles: one seemed fairly prosaic apart from the word "hunchback", while the other seemed more like the title of a fairy story or a fable, which made the following paragraphs more surprising.

The consideration of the content produced suggestions about the use of an outsider as the subject matter and of how sympathetically Thomas had presented "A solitary mister" compared with the selection of characters in 'The Mouse and the Woman'. Use of the first and third person narrator was also mentioned.

My students enjoyed discovering the links between the extracts (eg shared vocabulary) as well as ideas of personification, sound, oppression, movement, violence, place and feeling.

Metaphors and similes were discussed, especially the seemingly simple ones. They noted the hunchback "'Propped between trees and water", "'Like the water he sat down'" his running "On out of sound". In 'The Mouse and the Woman' the trees which "waved green hands over the wall to the world outside" and the "sweet expression" of the building produced quality analysis and a concentration on how Thomas was able to make language work.

As a result of this exercise, students felt that they were getting to grips with the actual work of Thomas and that they were able to make intelligent and useful comments on style, content and approach.

Ways through 70 poems

COLLECTION BY COLLECTION

As a way of breaking down the daunting mass of seventy poems to be studied, I have found it useful to tackle all the poems in *Selected Poems* collection by collection and thus to provide students with a coherent path forward.

Doing this gives students a sense of completing a logical unit of work, progressing through a collection of poems which are held together by the fact of their publication in one volume originally.

In the list which follows the poems from *Selected Poems* are grouped according to the collections in which the poems first appeared.

18P - *18 Poems* (1934)
25P - *Twenty-five Poems* (1936)
ML - *The Map of Love* (1939)
DE - *Deaths and Entrances* (1946)
ICS - *In Country Sleep* (1952)
CP - *Collected Poems* (1952)

Details of early drafts of the listed poems can be found in the notes by Walford Davies in *Selected Poems* (Everyman, 1993). The page references refer to that same edition.

Page

18P	14	Before I knocked
18P	15	My hero bares his nerves
18P	17	Light breaks where no sun shines
18P	17	The force that through the green fuse
18P	21	When once the twilight locks
18P	22	Where once the waters of your face
18P	23	Our eunuch dreams
18P	25	I see the boys of summer
18P	27	If I were tickled by the rub of love
18P	28	Especially when the October wind

25P	5	Out of the sighs
25P	7	I have longed to move away
25P	8	And death shall have no dominion
25P	10	Ears in the turrets hear
25P	11	Here in this spring
25P	11	Why east wind chills
25P	12	The hand that signed the paper
25P	20	This bread I break
25P	29	Should lanterns shine
25P	30	'Altarwise' Sonnet I
25P	31	'Altarwise' Sonnet IV
25P	31	Incarnate devil

ML	2	The spire cranes
ML	9	We lying by seasand
ML	32	How shall my animal
ML	32	O make me a mask
ML	34	After the funeral (In memory of Ann Jones)
ML	34	When all my five and country senses
ML	36	The tombstone told
ML	37	On no work of words
ML	37	Twenty-four years
ML	38	If my head hurt a hair's foot
ML	38	Once it was the colour of saying

DE	39	To Others than You
DE	40	When I woke
DE	41	Paper and sticks
DE	42	There was a saviour
DE	43	Deaths and Entrances
DE	44	On the Marriage of a Virgin
DE	45	Ballad of the Long-legged Bait
DE	51	Love in the Asylum
DE	52	The hunchback in the park
DE	53	Among those Killed in the Dawn Raid was a Man Aged a Hundred
DE	54	Lie still, sleep becalmed

DE   55   Ceremony After a Fire Raid

DE   58   Poem in October

DE   60   Holy Spring

DE   61   The conversation of prayers

DE   62   A Refusal to Mourn the Death, by
          Fire, of a Child in London

DE   63   This side of the truth (for Llewelyn)

DE   64   A Winter's Tale

DE   68   In my craft or sullen art

DE   69   Fern Hill

DE   70   On a Wedding Anniversary

ICS   71   In Country Sleep

ICS   74   Over Sir John's hill

ICS   76   In the White Giant's Thigh

ICS   78   Lament

ICS   80   Do not go gentle into that good night

ICS   81   Poem on his Birthday

CP   1   Prologue

CP   84   Elegy (added as an appendix in
         printings after 1956)

The following poems were not published in collections during Dylan Thomas's lifetime. Many are, however, available in his notebooks which were edited by Ralph Maud and first published as *Poet in the Making: The Notebooks of Dylan Thomas* (Dent, 1968).

Page

3   Being but men

6   Out of a war of wits

7   Their faces shone under some
    radiance

13   That sanity be kept

16   Song (Love me, not as the
     dreaming nurses)

18   A letter to my Aunt

57   Last night I dived my beggar arm

58   Poem (Your breath was shed)

THEMES

When talking about themes in Dylan Thomas's writings, there is a fair leeway when placing a poem in a particular category: some poems could fit (or be made to fit) virtually any category that you care to think about. Any list of themes is, of course, open to qualification, amendment and development.

During a recent classroom discussion my students suggested the following list of thematic categories:

Poetry	Welshness
Birth	Rhetoric
Death	Creativity
Love	Nature
Sex	Politics
Religion	Writing
Age	Childhood
Progress	Creation
Time	Destruction
Growth	Family
Development	Relationships
Landscape	

From this list I prepared a grid, listing poems along one axis and themes along the other, and invited my students to fill in the grid by indicating links between poems and themes. There are, of course, many poems that explore more than one theme as indicated in the entries opposite.

	Poetry	Wales	Nature	Land-scape	Religion	Sex	Place	Creativity	Love	Birth/Death
Prologue	✔	✔	✔							
The spire cranes	✔									
Being but men			✔					✔		
Out of the sighs						✔			✔	
Out of a war of wits	✔							✔		
Their faces shone under some radiance						✔				✔
I have longed to move away					✔			✔		✔
And death shall have no dominion					✔					✔
We lying by seasand			✔	✔					✔	

I think it is important that students be allowed to construct the thematic categories for their own grids in an exercise of this kind so that they feel ownership of their perceptions of how the poems could be arranged.

The grid which appears on pages 16-17 has been prepared so that it can be photocopied for use by students; in my view, it is the process of categorising poems which is important rather than the final shape of the argument.

	T	h	e	m	e	s			
Prologue									
The spire cranes									
Being but men									
Out of the sighs									
Out of a war of wits									
Their faces shone under some radiance									
I have longed to move away									
And death shall have no dominion									
We lying by seasand									
Ears in the turrets hear									
Here in this spring									
Why east wind chills									
The hand that signed the paper									
That sanity be kept									
Before I knocked									
My hero bares his nerves									
Song (Love me, not as the dreaming nurses)									
The force that through the green fuse									
Light breaks where no sun shines									
A letter to my Aunt									
This bread I break									
When once the twilight locks									
Where once the water of your face									
Our eunuch dreams									
I see the boys of summer									
If I were tickled by the rub of love									
Especially when the October wind									
Should lanterns shine									
'Altarwise' Sonnet I									
'Altarwise' Sonnet IV									
Incarnate devil									
O make me a mask									
How shall my animal									
When all my five and country senses									

DYLAN THOMAS's
Selected Poems

	T	h	e	m	e	s		
After the funeral (In memory of Ann Jones)								
The tombstone told								
On no work of words								
Twenty-four years								
Once it was the colour of saying								
If my head hurt a hair's foot								
To Others than You								
When I woke								
Paper and sticks								
There was a saviour								
Deaths and Entrances								
On the Marriage of a Virgin								
Ballad of the Long-legged Bait								
Love in the Asylum								
The hunchback in the park								
Among those Killed in the Dawn Raid was a Man Aged a Hundred								
Lie still, sleep becalmed								
Ceremony After a Fire Raid								
Last night I dived my beggar arm								
Poem (Your breath was shed)								
Poem in October								
Holy Spring								
The conversation of prayers								
A Refusal to Mourn the Death, by Fire, of a Child in London								
This side of the truth (for Llewelyn)								
A Winter's Tale								
In my craft or sullen art								
Fern Hill								
On a Wedding Anniversary								
In Country Sleep								
Over Sir John's hill								
In the White Giant's Thigh								
Lament								
Do not go gentle into that good night								
Poem on his Birthday								
Elegy								

Approaches to individual poems

In the pages which follow I have chosen to comment on six poems from *Selected Poems*: each was printed in a different collection of Dylan Thomas's work during the poet's lifetime.

I do not attempt to give a full description of each chosen poem with full annotation – I assume that other, and more exhaustive, academic text books will be used to explain the detail of the influences and allusions that the poems contain. My concern is to outline approaches that have worked in my classroom.

There are obviously many classroom approaches that will work for poetry which must be linked to individual classes and students; I am merely presenting poems which have worked for me and which have stimulated students to produce interesting and involved work which shows understanding and some enjoyment.

'PROLOGUE'
Collected Poems, 1952

Approaches

- Response to Thomas quotation from letter

- Class discussion

- Group annotation and sharing of photocopied text

Thomas worked long and hard on this poem specifically to be used as the prologue to his *Collected Poems*; it therefore seems logical to use the poem as a prologue to the study of the poems in the *Selected Poems*. Although a late poem, Thomas described it in a letter as "not dense, elliptical verse, but (fairly)

straightforward and colloquial", and, therefore, taking him at his words, a poem which will allow students a less threatening introduction to Thomas's verse than some of the other poems in the collection.

As a starting-point the class was given the following extract from a letter where Thomas says:

[The Prologue is] addressed to the (maybe) readers of the *Collected Poems*, & full (I hope) of references to my methods of work, my aims, & the kind of poetry I want to write.
(*Letter to David Higham, June 1952*)

Concentrating on the phrases "methods of work", "aims" and "kind of poetry", the class was encouraged to speculate on what these phrases might mean. As a result of general class discussion, they suggested a series of questions of which the following three lines of investigation were taken for further consideration:

What evidence is there in 'Prologue' of his "methods of work"?

What aims are outlined in 'Prologue'?

What effects are achieved in 'Prologue' by the poet's use of language, rhyme, rhythm and imagery?

The poem was then read in class. A short general discussion outlining the task ahead followed, and then the class was divided into three groups. Each group was given a photocopy of the poem on one sheet of A3 paper. The three questions outlined above were written at the top of the page. Each group was given one of the three questions to consider, annotating the sheet with their comments. At the end of ten minutes the sheet was passed on to the next group with the question that they had considered ticked off. The next group considered the next question and annotated the sheet, and so on until the last question. At the end of thirty minutes each of the sheets had a series of annotations and the groups reported back to the whole class about what they had discovered.

The last question, with its focus on language, rhyme, rhythm and imagery, proved to be the most productive. The sheet of responses included comments on word play, alliteration, dialect, exclamations, compound words, slang, use of vowels, striking images, animal sounds, landscape, Wales, biblical imagery and so on, though Thomas's rhyming structure within 'Prologue' was not picked up at this early stage.

As discussion and reporting back progressed so further annotations were added to the A3 sheets.

Each student was then given a clean A3 sheet of the poem and, again in groups, using their group sheets, each student made their own annotated version of the poem.

This sheet was then used as a point of reference for the poems studied later and could be amended in the light of further experience of the poems.

I have found that 'Prologue' can also be used as an epilogue at the end of a study of Dylan Thomas's poems as in the assignment which follows:

Read through the following extract from Thomas's 'Poetic Manifesto' and then consider how far this description of his poetic methods applies to 'Prologue' and to other poems in *Selected Poems*.

"I am a painstaking, conscientious, involved and devious craftsman in words, however unsuccessful the result so often appears, and to whatever wrong uses I may apply my technical paraphernalia, I use everything and anything to make my poems work and move in the directions I want them to: old tricks, new tricks, puns, portmanteau-words, paradox, allusion, paranomasia [paronomasia], paragram, catacheresis, slang, assonantal rhymes, vowel rhymes, sprung rhythm. Every device there is in language is there to be used if you will. Poets have got to enjoy themselves sometimes, and the twistings and convolutions of words, the inventions and contrivances, are all part of the joy that is part of the painful, voluntary work."

'Poetic Manifesto', *Texas Quarterly*, Winter 1961 [1951]

'ONCE IT WAS THE COLOUR OF SAYING'

The Map of Love, 1939

- Turning points and changes

- Memory and perception

- Highlighted areas of difficulty and understanding

- Form

For many students this was a frustrating poem: much of it seemed very clear to them and then they came up against phrases which did not seem to fit.

The starting point was a discussion of turning points:

What have been the turning points in your life?

How did you recognise them?

How did you deal with them?

What have you said about them?

Developing from this was a discussion about memory and the way that our perception of people, places and things changes over time – both for good and bad. Students were able to offer experiences which showed a progression in their approach to life.

The poem was presented via an overhead projector with the lines which were clearly understandable underlined in one colour and those that were 'difficult' underlined in another. Concentration on the accessible lines produced a range of responses connected with memory and experience: "uglier side of a hill", "gentle seaslides", "black and white patch of girls", "we stoned the cold and cuckoo/Lovers in the dirt" were phrases which gained an immediate response. They responded to the pun of "capsized" and liked the use of the slang word "mitching".

From the known they attempted to come to terms with the difficult, and in groups worked on the concept of a poet talking about the writing that has been done and the writing that will be completed in the future.

They also made the discovery that perhaps it was not necessary to understand everything in a poem literally, and that some lines might not be capable of exact interpretation – at least not by this teacher.

'IN MY CRAFT OR SULLEN ART'
Deaths and Entrances, 1946

Approaches

- Group work - brainstorming
    What is a poet?
    Why do poets write?

- Empathy with a creative impulse

- Response to the title

- Marking key words about poetry and creativity

- Detailed analysis

- Imaginative work - letter to a friend

When confronted by the question, "Why does a poet bother to write poems?" a whole series of responses was produced which included the following:

to show off

to be clever

to get published

to make 'us' suffer.

This led on to a sharing of personal experiences about poetry writing. For the vast majority of the group the only poetry writing that had been attempted had been as a direct result of teacher led assignments, and the results of those experiences were related with a mixture of embarrassment and resentment. Only one student admitted to writing poetry as a voluntary and necessary part of her creative life. She did share her reasons and was able to lead the discussion into the difficult area of how students manage to express their inmost thoughts and emotions. The group managed to articulate a whole series of "ways of getting things out":

going out and having a good time

sport

hobbies

music

dancing

letter writing

gossiping with friends

talking with parents.

The importance of expressing feelings was admitted and the difficulties were graphically explained in a revealing series of anecdotal reminiscences!

It was against this background that 'In my craft or sullen art' was considered. The title was discussed emphasising the differences between the words "craft" and "art". The implications of the word "sullen" were also considered and later analysis of the poem came back time, and again, to what the word suggested.

The importance of the effort that Thomas puts into his poetry as expressed in this poem was appreciated and students responded especially strongly to the following lines:

  "I labour by singing light"
where the image was felt to be strong and to be achieved in language which presented a complex idea in simple language;

  "Not for ambition or bread"
where the simplicity was felt to be almost Messianic, and

  "Who pay no praise or wages
  Nor heed my craft or art"
where the archaic texture of the line was felt to give an almost timeless sense to the predicament of the artist.

I asked the students to write a short letter from the poet to a friend based on the sentiments expressed in the poem, explaining how the poet felt about what he was doing. This was a productive exercise as the students were able to identify with Thomas in what he was having difficulty with as they were struggling with his poetry. They were able to sympathise with his predicament as they were able to relate his feelings of frustration and lack of worth with their own efforts.

Read through the comments of the critics and consider the questions below.

Do you fully understand what the critics are saying?

What sort of language is the critic using?

What tone is the critic using?

Who do you think these comments are intended for?

What is the attitude of the critic towards the poet?

What is the attitude of the critic towards the reader?

How helpful do you think these comments are?

Which critic would you be interested in reading further?

"His voice resembles no other voice; the spirit is that of the beginning of created things: there is here no case of a separate imagination of invention. From the depths of Being, from the roots of the world, a voice speaks."

Edith Sitwell, *The Atlantic Book of British and American Poetry* (Little, Brown and Co, 1958)

"Drunk with melody, and what the words were he cared not."

Robert Graves, *The Crowning Privilege* (Cassell, 1955)

"All the same, there is still a lot of his poetry where I can feel it works and yet can't see why. I have no theory at all about the meaning of the line: "The two-a-vein, the foreskin, and the cloud," though I am sure there is a reason why it seems very good; and indeed I don't much like the poem (called "Now") it's the last line of, so I don't bother about it, but I assume on principle there is something there which I feel and can't see, but could see."

William Empson, *Collected Poems and Under Milk Wood* (New Statesman, 1954) quoted in C B Cox, *Dylan Thomas: A Collection of Critical Essays* (Prentice-Hall, 1966)

"Words, single words, are far more important in Thomas's poetry than in that of Yeats or Auden. We should expect this. Although Auden has said that a "passionate love of words" is a pre-requisite for every poet, his own highly referential language depends much more on that "natural momentum of syntax" which Yeats sought for so diligently, than on the individual word. The norm of both Yeats's and Auden's poetry is fluency, conversation: the norm of Thomas's is incantation, the single word as thing, dropped on to the page."

John Bayley, *Dylan Thomas* (Constable, 1957) quoted in C B Cox ibid.

"A problem in interpreting some of Thomas's poems will consist in determining which movement from which darkness to which light is being described. Suppose, for example, that he seems to be following, with obstetrical manual at hand, the progress of an organism through its ovular, embryonic, and fetal stages to birth. Is his subject no more than this? No, he may be exploring the relation between phylogeny and ontogeny, or microcosm and macrocosm. Or the progress of the organism may offer a narrative structure for the working out of social, psychological, or moral judgements. And if the organism happens to be Christ, an entirely new dimension is added, and the additional question of whether Christ is a member of the Trinity, a facsimile of Lawrence's *Man Who Died*, an epitome of all the fertility-deities in *The Golden Bough*, or Thomas raised to the nth degree."

Clark Emery, *The World of Dylan Thomas* (Dent, 1971)

But one thing seems clear. The more dilute and 'open' Thomas's later style becomes, the more nakedly will this question of his beliefs, or the general question of his 'ideas' or feelings appear. The textural difficulty of an earlier poem deflects attention from the nature of its thought or implications, or at least delays attention to these things. And in the end what it adds up to is a concrete narrative, not a conceptual statement with which we might agree or disagree, or find adequate or inadequate. In this way, paradoxically, it is the later poems which run the greater risks perhaps.

Walford Davies, *Dylan Thomas* (Open University Press, 1986)

I have found that there is an understandable reluctance on the part of students (and teachers) to share particularly useful sources of information. However, it is essential that the study of literature in the classroom is a collaborative exercise with students and teachers feeling themselves part of the same exploration; it is therefore only fair that the 'maps' are shared!

I encourage my students to share their experiences of their use of critics and to explain to the group why one critic has been of more use to them than another. A pooling of resources that they had found useful is also of benefit to all.

The critical bibliography at the end of this booklet gives the results of student and teacher evaluation.

Above: Dylan Thomas in 1937
© Dylans Bookstore

Left: Dylan Thomas sent this photograph to Vernon Watkins in 1938
© Dylans Bookstore

Top: Dylan and Caitlin Thomas, 1937
© Dylans Bookstore

Above: Dylan Thomas in New York,
1933 © Dylans Bookstore

Left: Rare stills of Dylan Thomas on
television, 1953 © Dylans Bookstore